# SEVEN SECRETS TO UNLEASHING YOUR FULL POTENTIALS

*By*
*LUCKY FLOURISH*

Copyright 2022 Lucky Flourish.

All rights reserved. No part of the publication may be reproduced, distributed, or transmitted in any form or by any means, including photocopying, recording, or other electronic or mechanical methods, without the prior written permission of the publisher, except in the of brief quotations embodied in critical reviews and certain other non-commercial uses permitted by copyright law.For permission requests, contact the publisher through the contacts below.

Front cover image by Flucky Artist
Book Design by Flucky Artist

Address: Ilorin, Kwara State.
Phone Number:+2349130098974
Email Address:
flourishabisola987@gmail.com

*Sincerely,*

*Lucky Flourish,*

*A Writer.*

# TABLE OF CONTENTS

# CHAPTER 1

# INTRODUCTION

*WHAT ARE POTENTIALS?*

latent qualities or abilities that may be developed and lead to future success or usefulness.
existing in possibility : capable of development into actuality
something that can develop or become actual
Potential can be either good or bad. Studying hard increases the potential for success, but wet roads increase the potential for accidents. But when a person or thing "has potential", we always expect something good from it in the future.

the possibility of
something developing or happening in
a particular way:

have the potential for sth/to do sth *These equity securities are believed to have the potential for high earnings growth.*

How to Find Your Potential

1. Identify Your Inner Voice. The first step towards success is to listen to yourself. ...
2. Make Conscious Efforts. Once you've planned a suitable final destination, it's time to make an effort. ...
3. Define Your Goals. ...
4. Set Milestones. ...
5. Accept Failures. ...
6. Celebrate Your Successes.

*If you want to unleash your full potentials, then check out these ways:*

# CHAPTER 2

## DISCOVER YOUR PURPOSE.

Finding your purpose means finding a way to impact the world in a way that fulfills and satisfies you. Your purpose aligns with your dreams, your values and your actions. It gives meaning to your existence.

The first thing you need is to have a direction for where you really want to go. In order to do this, you need to discover first what is the purpose of your life—why you exist. The only one who can answer this is God, your creator, so you need to draw closer to Him to learn more about His will and plans for your life.

*12 STEPS TO DISCOVER YOUR PURPOSE*

If you find yourself shuffling through your 20's, 30's, 40's (or even later) and feeling the disappointment of not knowing your life purpose, be assured there's still time.

You may be surprised to discover you actually have more in common with Julia Child, Vincent van Gogh, JK Rowling and Oprah than you realized, because as these highly successful and purpose-filled people eventually figured out, your dreams have no age limit — and neither does your souls purpose.

Most of us struggle to know what we want to do with our lives, even if we've already finished school, got a job, changed careers, met our life partner or had children.

The length of time or number of attempts and reattempts it takes to discover your 'calling' isn't the issue. The problem lays in the possibility of regret — in never having acknowledged what our purpose might be and then acted on it.

Finding your purpose means finding a way to impact the world in a way that fulfills and satisfies you. Your purpose aligns with your dreams, your values and your actions.

*It gives meaning to your existence.*

Mark Twain famously declared that "the two most important days in your life are the day you are born and the day you find out why."

So how *do* you find out why you were born?

1. Trust that you really do have a higher purpose

Just because you haven't discovered it yet, it doesn't mean you won't! Don't beat yourself up. Instead, see any 'wrong turns' as an opportunity to figure out what you *don*t want. Know that some of the most purpose-filled people are those who have reinvented themselves time and time again.


2. Listen to your inner knowing

Learning to find and then live your purpose can be an inside job. You need to do a little soul-searching. So go somewhere you can sit without distraction and connect with yourself in a way that works for you. Journal. Meditate. Speak to someone you trust. Just get out of your head and into your heart — this is where you'll be guided to the answer.

Identify your passions, your values, and your goals

3. Take action, every day

Once you begin to hone in on your passions, values and goals, work on aligning them with your actions. Commit to honoring them as best you can, every day. How can you take action right now, even on a small scale? Once you start taking inspired action, notice how it feels.

Passion is the key to a purposeful life. When you are inspired and connected to what brings you joy, you find the motivation to create and experience even more of what lights you up.

Think about your answers from our purpose-exploring exercise and connect them to the idea of helping others. How can you use your purpose to leave a lasting effect on the world? Is there an issue you care about? How can you start to solve it? You may not fix all of humanity's problems on your own, but you can contribute. Making a difference can be fulfilling.

According to Jess Lively jesslively.com the equation for finding your purpose is this:

Your Talent + Helping People = Purpose.

Jess believes your purpose is always to help others in whatever way you can — in this present moment.

4. Don't just make it about money

If you can channel your calling into a career, then great! However, living on-purpose can be achieved in many ways — it doesn't have to be in your job or the way you make a living.

In his well-known narrative, Alan Watts encourages you to do what you desire or what makes you itch — and forget about the money:

"If you say that getting the money is the most important thing, you will spend your life completely wasting your time. You'll be doing things you don't like doing in order to go on living — that is to go on doing things you don't like doing — which is stupid," he says.

## 5. Define your own version of success

Success is really about living life on-purpose. No one, however well-meaning, can tell you what that purpose is or what you should be doing. Do not live your own life by someone else definition of success.

## 1. SEARCH INWARD

The questions "What is my purpose in life?" and "How can I be happy?" are actually the same — and they have the same answer. You can never truly understand how to find your purpose by listening to others' opinions and seeking outside approval.

Everything you need is within yourself. The only thing holding you back is your own limiting beliefs. With each limiting belief you identify and replace with an empowering belief, you develop greater self-awareness. And when you're in control of your emotions, you're in control of your life.

## 2. PUT PURPOSE BEFORE GOALS

If you focus only on achieving short-term goals, you will never find your true passion or learn how to find your purpose. The goals you work toward must always be based on finding your purpose. If they're not, you'll only feel a fleeting sense of accomplishment and will soon be seeking something more. You won't be able to see that life is happening *for* you instead of *to* you.

When you set a goal, ask yourself: How will this help me feel more fulfilled? How does this relate back to my purpose? Use a journal or a system like Tony's Rapid Planning Method to ensure you always keep your purpose top of mind.

## 3. FOCUS ON WHAT YOU HAVE

Developing an abundance mindset is like opening your eyes to life: You will see beauty and goodness all around you. With this new perspective, your purpose in life becomes much clearer. You question less and less how to find your purpose because you feel like you have more of the answers and that you are on the path to achieving meaningful goals.

When we focus on what we have, fear disappears and abundance appears. You'll stop living in fear that you're wasting your life and begin to attract positivity and joy. Finding your purpose becomes an exciting journey, rather than a stressful goal.

## 4. TAKE OWNERSHIP OF YOUR LIFE

True fulfillment comes from designing your own life. This is how you unlock the extraordinary. To find your purpose, you must decide what's truly right, and know it in your heart and soul. You must not let yourself be driven by fear or anxiety. A decision made from fear is always the wrong decision. It will not help you understand "What is my purpose?" but instead confuse the issue even more.

To truly take ownership, you must stop playing the victim. Realize that every circumstance in your life is a result of your own decisions, not anyone else's. When you take responsibility for finding your purpose instead of blaming others, fulfillment follows.

## 5. THINK ABOUT WHAT BRINGS YOU JOY

Look back on your life and identify the times when you felt the most joy. Was it when you were connecting with your partner? Making a successful presentation at work? Creating art or helping others? When you discover what brings you joy, you usually discover where your passions lie.

Your abilities are connected to that sense of joy, so examine them, too: Can you pick up a pencil and sketch a lifelike portrait? Do your friends tell you that you're a great listener? When you look closely at the activities or skills that come naturally and also bring you joy, you'll likely stumble upon passions that you can turn into a profitable career.

## 6. DEVELOP YOUR OWN LIFE VISION STATEMENT

Before you can ask yourself "What is my purpose?" you first have to know what an ideal world looks like and how you fit into it. Creating a life vision statement involves identifying what life would look like if everyone were living up to their fullest potential. This will help you develop a road map to guide you in the proper direction.

## 7. DISCOVER YOUR TRUE NEEDS

When asking themselves "What is my purpose in life?", some people don't even know where to start. If you fall into this category, it helps to examine the Six Human Needs. Your top need – certainty, significance, variety, love/connection, growth or contribution – affects every decision you make.

Lack of awareness about your own needs can leave you with a false sense of purpose – one that is actually based on others' expectations. This is why you can reach the top of the career ladder, find the "perfect" partner or be in the best shape of your life, but still not feel happy. Fulfillment begins with your innermost needs.

## 8. WRITE OUT YOUR STORY

Writing helps us organize our thoughts – and discover new ones we may not even know we had. It's proven to help us reach goals, improve memory and decrease stress, which are all essential when you're learning how to find your purpose.

Putting your life in writing can reveal hidden meanings you may not see otherwise. Start with this exercise: What strengths do you have that helped you get through tough times? How have you helped others? And how have other people helped you? Write it all down and you'll begin to see patterns that will help you find your purpose.

## 9. TAKE TIME FOR YOURSELF

"What is my purpose?" is a deep question that takes time and reflection to answer. When you spend all your time running from one commitment to another, you never have time to just sit quietly and reconnect with yourself. Make sure you schedule enough personal time to reduce the noise and demands of the outer world and focus on what you want.

When you feel depleted searching for meaning in life, take a deep breath and center yourself. Take time for  self-care, whether that's a spa day or reading a book in the park. It's by looking within that you're able to identify your values – the beliefs you hold most dear as a guiding force in life. You won't understand how to find your purpose without first taking a step back and relaxing.

## 10. EMBRACE ACCEPTANCE

Part of finding your purpose is accepting your own limitations. Instead of getting frustrated with yourself, give yourself a break. Get to know yourself bit by bit, taking the role of observer. As you practice self-compassion while building self-awareness, you're able to find the meaning you're seeking.

Self-compassion means being patient with yourself. Feeling lost in life can be a very disorienting feeling. You may feel frustrated, but be gentle with yourself. Everyone who has ever asked themselves "What is my purpose?" began from a place of uncertainty. Their hesitancy was what prompted them to dig deep and find greater meaning.

## 11. FIND YOUR COMMUNITY

Finding your purpose in life is often about discovering where you fit in. When we meet our "people," we feel like we are home: relaxed and at ease, able to truly be ourselves. Your community can often help you discover how to find your purpose, or to live your purpose once you've found it.

To find your community, follow your passions. Join a volunteer group. Take a class to develop a skill you enjoy. Seek out support online. Find others who enjoy the same music, books or plays. The saying "You are who your friends are" is true – and when you find the right community, it's a good thing.

## 12. BE FLEXIBLE

One of the hardest parts of learning how to find your purpose is letting go of old identities and interests that no longer serve us. Yet it's something that must be done. Your purpose in life is also likely to grow and change as you grow and change. You must be willing to be flexible and to listen to your innermost wants and needs.

Finding your purpose is a lifelong journey. Being flexible lets you grow in integrity while being true to yourself. When you develop your core values and stop seeking external affirmation, you'll find that the question of "What is my purpose in life?" is much easier to answer.

Research shows that finding your purpose is linked to living longer. Researchers surveyed nearly 7,000 older adults on the relationship between mortality and finding your purpose. Participants who did not have a strong sense of meaning in their lives were more than twice as likely to die prematurely as those who had figured out their purpose in life. Having a sense of purpose also reduced the incidence of cardiovascular events like heart attack and stroke.

These results were universal, even when controlled for income, race, gender and education level. Researchers concluded that finding your purpose helps you live longer. It's also essential for happiness and fulfillment.

Achieving goals may not help you find the purpose of life, but knowing your purpose can help you achieve your goals. When you truly know your purpose, you'll experience a sense of clarity like never before as you're able to connect what you want to achieve to your ultimate fulfillment. You'll feel passionate, driven and laser-focused. You'll stop battling with the past and the future and start living in the present – and that's the greatest gift you can give yourself.

# CHAPTER 3

## SET GOALS.

*What is goal setting?*

Some people may have trouble sticking to goals because they don't distinguish their goals from more casual, everyday self-improvement efforts. Just because you decide to start running every day doesn't necessarily make that a conscious goal. So let's revisit what goal setting means.

Goal setting is a purposeful and explicit process that starts with identifying a new objective, skill, or project you want to achieve. Then, you make a plan for achieving it, and you work to complete it.

Instead of just running with no particular purpose, a true goal would be more along the lines of starting a training program to complete a specific race, say a Thanksgiving Day half marathon, which requires much more careful planning, motivation, and discipline.

Goal setting is a purposeful and explicit process that starts with identifying a new objective, skill, or project you want to achieve. Then, you make a plan for achieving it, and you work to complete it.

Why is goal setting important?

When you set goals, you take control of your life's—or your work's—direction. Goals provide you with focus. The decisions you make and actions you take should bring you closer to achieving those goals.

Setting goals keeps you moving, increases your happiness, and significantly benefits your organization. When you set goals, you create a vision of what your life or your business could look like. Then you start pushing yourself and your team to get the best results possible.

What is goal-setting theory?

Proposed by industrial-organizational psychologist Edwin Locke, goal-setting theory recommends how to set the most effective kinds of goals. Locke found that employees perform better and are more motivated to complete goals if those goals are difficult.

In other words, you can't cheat. The easier the goal, the less you'll work to achieve it. If you set hard (but not impossible) goals, you'll actually put in the highest level of effort.

This article goes into detail on the other important aspects of Locke's theory, like setting realistic goals and being self-motivated. Keep reading to get the most out of your personal goals or have your employees be effective when setting their own.

"If you want to be happy, set a goal that commands your thoughts, liberates your energy and inspires your hopes." – Andrew Carnegie.

When we are faced with difficult times as we are now with the effects of a worldwide pandemic, it is easy to get discouraged and lose hope.  Hope is a vital component of human existence, and it is needed to find happiness and peace during times that might otherwise lead us to be discouraged.  As Andrew Carnegie so clearly pointed out, setting a goal can keep your thoughts focused, direct your energy, and inspire the hope that is needed to move through and beyond a moment of despair.

Have you ever wondered why some people are so good at fulfilling their dreams and living a life of purpose? What is their "secret sauce" for success?

Some people would say that all you need to do is work hard to achieve what you want in life. Some people think it's about who you know or what you have.  Yet others feel there are those born with access and that they are given all the breaks in life.  The truth is, statistics demonstrate that those who create goals and have a regular and consistent goal-setting process are much more likely to achieve their life's dreams.

Regardless of how hard you work, if you are aiming for the wrong dream, then all that effort will only get you to the wrong destination faster, and that would be extremely disappointing.

Despite connections, you still have to continuously demonstrate to everyone that you were worthy of receiving the opportunity in the first place.  Eventually, proving your worth to others becomes exhausting.

However, there is a formula for turning your dreams into reality, and it isn't dependent on who you know or proving yourself.  The formula is:

 goals + commitment = dreams come true

By having clear goals, you become aware of precisely what you want to achieve and how to go about doing it. You are able to more accurately assess and measure your ability to accomplish the goals and most importantly, you have a plan that can guide you along the way and keep you on track.

Add commitment and determination to your goals and you will find that you are willing to take continuous and consistent action toward making your dreams a reality, despite any obstacles in your path, including difficult times.

Having goals and staying committed to them will keep your focus on the things that you have identified as essential to reaching your desired outcomes.  Too often, we expend precious time on issues that have nothing to do with what we really want in our lives. We get distracted by focusing on what others are doing and achieving, and striving to do the same.

Having a vision and a supporting plan of what you want to achieve in life is necessary if you ever want to arrive at the correct destination.

We know that this is a very difficult time and staying focused during the COVID-19 pandemic can definitely be a challenge.  We also know that life will continue for the vast majority of people during and after this pandemic.  Now, more than ever, we believe that it is important to stay focused on something that can drive you through this difficult time.  Because of this, we've put together a Goal-Setting Guide to help you get on track to achieving goals and manifesting your life's dreams.

That's why we are providing a Goal Setting Toolkit to help you identify your goals and create a plan to keep you on track. We hope that it will help motivate and encourage you to stay focused on your goals and develop a plan to reach your life's dreams, even during this difficult time.

Along the way to discovering your purpose, it is important that you set the goals that you want to achieve within a span of time. You can create short-term goals, like being able to finish a book within a week, or long-term goals, such as establishing your business in five years.

*How to set goals in 7 steps*

If goals are so important, <u>why do we fail to achieve them</u>? Because we don't plan the steps to get there.

A goal setting process forces you to think about the journey (in other words, how you're going to complete your tasks) instead of just the end destination. Take a look at the steps below to get started.

1. Think about the results you want to see

Before you set a goal, take a closer look at what you're trying to achieve and ask yourself the following questions:

- Is this goal something you truly want?
- Is it important enough to pour hours of time and effort into it?

If you're not willing to put in the time, it may not be worth pursuing.

If you create a long list of goals to pursue all at the same time, you may have a difficult time achieving any of them. Instead, use the questions above to determine which goals matter the most to you right now, and then focus on those few.

2. Create SMART goals

Once you've zeroed in on what you actually want, ensure your goal meets the SMART criteria:

- Specific
- Measurable
- Attainable
- Realistic
- Time-bound

The most important part of SMART goal setting is to make your goal specific so you can clearly track your progress and know whether you met the goal. The more specific you can be with your goal, the higher the chance you'll complete it.

For example, many people set goals to lose weight, but they don't always decide how much weight they want to lose and when they want to accomplish this goal. A specific goal would be "I want to lose 25 pounds by the Fourth of July." This goal provides an exact amount of weight to lose and an end date to do it by.

## 3. Write your goals down

When you write your goals down, they become real and tangible instead of a vague idea that resides only in your mind. Once you've written your goals down, keep them somewhere visible--put personal goals up on your mirror or near your computer screen, put team goals up on the walls next to everyone's desks, and include company goals in internal presentations.

This tactic reminds you to keep working on your goals daily. As you're writing down your goals, use a positive tone so you stay excited about completing them.

## 4. Create an action plan

Many people decide on a goal but never create an action plan to determine how exactly they will meet that goal. Your action plan should include the overall goal you're trying to meet and all the steps you need to take to get there.

Don't be afraid to get creative with your action plan. Go back to your elementary school days, and get creative. Write out your goal using crayons, markers, or colored pencils, for example. According to Forbes, creating an action plan this way activates a different part of your brain and cements the goals in your mind.

5. Create a timeline

As part of your action plan, use a timeline maker to help visualize roles, tasks, milestones, and deadlines to achieve your goal. Once you've set those dates, try to stick to them as closely as possible. A timeline creates a sense of urgency, which in turn motivates you to stay on schedule and finish your goal.

6. Take action

Now that you've planned everything out, it's time to take action. You didn't go through all that work just to forget about your goal. Every step that you take should lead to another until you finish your goal.

7. Re-evaluate and assess your progress

You need to keep your motivation strong to complete your goal. Consider scheduling a weekly evaluation, which could include measuring your progress and checking your schedule. Once you see how close the finish line is, you'll feel more motivated to push through to the end. If you're a little behind schedule, make necessary adjustments and keep going.

 Try to learn as many skills are possible.

Grab opportunities that will allow you to learn new skills. As availability and resources permit, enroll yourself in seminars or workshops that offer skill training. The more skills you have, the more bankable you become, plus you would never know when these skills would come in handy.

*Top 10 Strategies for Learning New Skills*

## 1. Ditch Your Learning Style

Are you a visual learner? Or is your learning style kinesthetic or auditory? I'll tell you a secret: you're none of these.

As much as we'd like to believe that we learn better in a certain style, the truth is, these have little impact on our ability to learn.

In an intriguing talk at TEDxUWLaCrosse, Dr. Tesia Marshik shares a startling fact: 40 years of research on learning styles has found that matching teaching styles to learning styles makes no difference at all. In her own experiments, Dr. Marshik found that students learned the same way, regardless of the way material was presented to them.

<u>Another study</u> was a little more blunt in its judgments:

> *The contrast between the enormous popularity of the learning-styles approach within education and the lack of credible evidence for its utility is, in our opinion, striking and disturbing.*

Yet the myth of learning styles persists, as a quick Google search will show you. So, what's really the best way to learn? It depends on what you're trying to learn in the first place.

For example, if you're trying to learn a new language, don't just read the textbook. Watch TV shows, listen to music, and converse with a native speaker through a <u>language exchange app</u>.

In an age where everything is available at the click of a button, there are many ways to learn. The key is to interact with the information. Using multiple sources will help you with this. Don't stick to books alone—gather relevant videos, podcasts, movies, and blogs as well!

## 2. Make It More Meaningful for Yourself

One main reason why "learning styles" don't work is that we learn things in terms of meaning. Finding meaning in our learning is the key.

A 1973 study by Chase and Simon illustrates this well. In the first part of the test, amateur and expert chess players were shown a chessboard arrangement from a game in progress and asked to recall the position of the pieces. While amateurs players could barely recall any of positions, the experts were able to recall most of them. The experts see the strategy, the meaning behind why the pieces are where they are.

In the second part, experts and amateurs were shown boards with the chess pieces arranged at random and asked to recall them. Both groups performed about equally. This time, the experts couldn't find any real connection or meaning in the way the pieces are arranged.

The same goes for learning. We all learned various facts and figures in school but how many of those do we actually remember? Only the information that was meaningful to us, that we've been able to connect to our own life and experiences.

If you try to force yourself to just memorize random facts, you're likely to forget them. Remember all those times you tried to memorize formulae without understanding their relevance? In order to make your learning stick, it's important to make real life connections and see how it fits in the larger scheme of things.

The next time you take a finance class, instead of memorizing a formula, try to understand what relevance it has in practice and how you can use it to your advantage. You'll find you're able to grasp the concepts much more quickly.

3. Learn by Doing

Humans are natural learners—and we learn best when we perform the tasks we're trying to learn. No matter how good your grades were at college, most of your learning takes place once you enter the workplace and start applying what you've learned.

Let's say you're trying to learn SEO. Don't invest all your time in learning the jargon and theory—dive in as soon as you can to master the skill through trial and error. Start a blog. Write a few posts. Find out for yourself what works and what doesn't. The more you do it, the more you learn.

Better yet, build new habits to enforce your new skills. Start small and reward yourself to start building a pattern of behavior that will reinforce what you're learning.

4. Study the Greats, and Then Practice

Aspiring writers hear over and over that the best way to write better is to read a lot of books, especially the classics. Why? Because they'll learn a lot more by studying the writing styles of great writers, than they would by taking a course on writing.

Let's take this advice a step further. While studying the greats is essential, it is more of a passive exercise. In order to gain from it, you need to apply that learning to your own work as well.

One way to do this is to mimic experts until you eventually develop your own style and technique. Benjamin Franklin taught himself to write this way, as he shares in his autobiography:

> *I took some of the papers (from The Spectator magazine), and, making short hints of the sentiment in each sentence, laid them by a few days, and then, without looking at the book, try'd to compleat the papers again, by expressing each hinted sentiment at length, and as fully as it had been expressed before, in any suitable words that should come to hand.*

On comparing his work with the originals, he found where he was lacking, and started turning the tales into poems and then back again. This is how he learned to express himself better.

This form of learning can be applied to any skill, be it writing, speaking another language, or even sports. Compare your work with that of experts in your field and you will notice areas that need improvement. Then, refer back to step 3 and keep practicing your skills. You will notice the difference.

## 5. Teach What You Learn

One of the more surprising ways you can learn a new skill is to teach it to someone else. Much research has been done on this phenomenon, but one study illustrates it particularly well.

In the study, two sets of participants study the same passage, with different expectations. One group was expected to teach it later, the other one expected a test on it. At the end, both groups were eventually tested on the material. Guess which group did better? Yep—the one that expected to teach it.

Why is this such an effective way to learn? Because when we learn with the intention to teach, we break the material down into simple, understandable chunks for ourselves. It also forces us to examine the topic more critically and thoroughly, helping us to understand it better.

You don't have to be an education major to use this trick. Try explaining what you're learning to friends or coworkers. If you're learning a new business software or skill, ask your boss if you can make a presentation to your team about it. See if you can field all their questions. Write regular blog posts or make vlogs while you're learning. See if you're able to express what you learn in simple words. The results might surprise you.

6. Spend More Time Practicing Things You Find Difficult

Practice in itself is great, but if you're practicing things you know well, you're doing it wrong. In order to excel at any skill, you need to push yourself out of your comfort zone and practice things you aren't good at. This is known as deliberate practice, and was popularized by Anders Ericsson.

Ericsson and his team studied expert athletes, violinists, and memory champions and found that they spent a lot of time improving areas they were weak. Additionally, they consulted their teachers to find out where exactly they were lacking.

Along with spending more time on your weaknesses, Ericsson also emphasizes the importance of concentration while practicing. If you're practicing while your mind is all over the place, you're not getting much out of it.

So the next time you sit to practice a new skill, step out of your comfort zone and challenge yourself. Concentrate on whatever is most difficult for you, and with time you'll find you achieve a higher level of overall efficiency.

7. Take Frequent Breaks

The brain has two modes—focused and diffused. For learning to happen, both modes are equally important.

While in focused mode, you're able to learn the nitty-gritty of a problem. In diffused mode, you're better able to see the big picture and bring it all together. You might have noticed this happening in the shower, when you're not focusing on anything in particular, then you suddenly remember a fact that was eluding you, or the solution to a problem.

It's important to let your brain relax for a while after a particularly intense session of study or practice, to give it time to connect the dots.

One good way to practice this is using the Pomodoro technique, which has you work on a project for 25 minutes, and then give yourself a 5 minute break. After four such sessions (that is, 100 minutes of work, with 15 minutes of break) you take another break for 15-30 minutes. This technique helps to keep your mind invigorated, and ensures you don't suffer mental fatigue.

Equally important is learning how to procrastinate productively, so your brain has time to truly recharge itself.


8. Test Yourself

We all loved to hate tests in school, but do you know just how effective they are in helping you learn? Turns out testing is one of the best ways to boost learning—even if you're simply practicing on your own, and not taking a high-stakes exam.

Testing even beats out methods such as re-reading and reviewing notes when it comes to making sure your learning sticks. An examination of the study techniques of top students by Elevate Education found that while most students re-read notes before exams, top students spend their time solving problems and taking practice exams.

Why is testing so effective? Because it takes recall a step further. Recall shows how much of the material you remember. Testing shows you how well you can use what you've learnt. After all, that is the ultimate goal of learning, isn't it?

9. Find A Mentor

Mentorship is perhaps the quickest way to take your skills to the next level. A mentor helps you navigate your field by offering invaluable perspective and experience.

Initially, look to friends, family, and coworkers for an expert in the skill you're trying to learn. If you come up with no one, start branching out your search to your larger community and industry.

When reaching out to experts, describe what you have to offer, rather than what you will gain. For example, maybe you could manage their social media accounts or help write their website content. Whatever services you can offer, be sure to let them know.

Business coach Michael Hyatt offers good advice about the ask:

*Though a true mentor may be difficult to find, it's not impossible. If you have one in mind, start by building the relationship—just like you would anyone else. Don't lead with "Will you be my mentor?" (That's like asking someone to marry you on the first date.) Instead, get to know them. Look for opportunities to be generous. Start small and see where it goes.*

The key is starting—the worst a person can do is say no, so ask!

## 10. Be Curious

Nothing stimulates learning quite like curiosity! So, as Ms. Frizzle from The Magic School bus famously said: "Ask questions, make mistakes, and get messy!"

Instead of letting a textbook guide your learning, you take the lead. Seek answers from many sources. Don't merely memorize theories and techniques—question them at every step. Think about why they matter, why they're relevant. Tinker with the tools and knowledge available. See what you end up discovering! You may end up surprising even yourself.

# CHAPTER 4

## FIND OUT HOW YOU CAN IMPROVE YOUR EXISTING TALENTS/SKILLS.

Do not settle with acquiring new skills. Taking your old talents to the next level will be a worthy investment. Upgraded skills can make you more in-demand in your career field.

*17 Motivating Ways to Improve Your Skills*

1. Find out what you are good at.

First, you need to identify what are the skills that you already possess—especially those that you want to improve. No matter how many skills you have, you need to pick your topmost expertise so you can focus on enhancing them.

2. Do not hide them.

Being shy is one of the reasons why a skill is usually left forgotten in a corner. If you want to improve your skills, then you need to come out of your closet and use them whenever and wherever needed. You need to get used to using them around people so that they can be beneficial to yourself and others.

3. Be involved in activities that will require them.

The more you use your skills, the more that they are honed. For this reason, do not miss opportunities that will allow you to showcase what you got there. For instance, if you are good at playing instruments, then be involved in a band that plays in events.

4. Enroll in short courses and training that can enhance them.

Look for short courses or workshops that will not only give you a certificate of completion but will train you to be more effective in handling your skills too. These can supply you with fresh knowledge about your specialties, which can help you level up.

5. Keep using them.

What you do not use, you will eventually lose. If you do not use your skills for a long time, there is a tendency that you will forget about them. Therefore, keep your skills active and growing by constantly using them, whether professionally or just for your personal satisfaction.

6. Practice, practice, and practice.

Aside from frequently using your skills, you need to be intentional in practicing them. Practice makes perfect, so if you want to improve your skills, then you need to allot a practice time for each those. It may not be possible to achieve perfection, but at least you can gain excellence.

7. Watch online video tutorials.

Another way to enhance your craft is by watching tutorials or workshops on YouTube and other sites that provide access to these resources. You can find channels and professionals who share tips and secrets on how to upgrade skills.

8. Learn from the experts.

Aside from YouTube, there are other online platforms, featuring experts, which can help you gain more knowledge about your skills. You can also read books from well-known individuals from your field. However, the best way to learn from experts is by working with them up close and being able to observe how they do things.

9. Be mentored by a pro.

Better than just observing professionals, you can ask them to mentor you. You will not only get the chance to see them using their skills, but they can willingly teach you their secrets of how they achieved mastery.

10. Do not be content with your current level.

Always be hungry for growth. Even if people look up to you for competence, do not think that you are already the best. There is always room for improvement, so take every opportunity to advance.

11. Ask others to help you evaluate your skills.

Evaluating the current status of your skills will help you find out what needs to be done so you can improve. Of course, if you want an unbiased evaluation, then you should involve other people who see you use them. They can be your family, friends, colleagues, or mentors.

12. Monitor your growth.

Aside from evaluation, regular monitoring can help you track your skills' progress. You can create a checklist of the developments that you want to see in a certain period. This is a tool that can help you figure out your strengths and weaknesses.

13. Take criticisms constructively.

If you receive not-so-positive comments regarding your abilities, do not take them personally. Instead, take them as constructive criticisms that can help you objectively evaluate your level. Use them as a motivation to improve.

14. Avoid comparing your growth with others.

Stop comparing the level of your skills with that of others. Do not measure your progress based on their progress because each person has his/her own pace of development. This will make you either jealously competitive or insecure.

15. Put your heart into whatever you do.

One of the best ways to improve your skills is by loving them. If you are passionate about what you do, then learn them by heart. Your dedication will make you more patient and persevering in honing your craft.

16. Give time and focus through consistency.

Make a 20-minute habit of practicing every day. You cannot learn it all in one sitting. Consistency is the difference between all-time greats and one-hit wonders. Remember, creating a routine can help you achieve your desired result.

17. Use them to serve God and others.

The Bible says that everything has been created through Christ and for Christ (Colossians 1:16). This means that talents, skills, knowledge, wisdom, and even spiritual gifts—if we acknowledge that they are from God—are meant to be used to serve Him and others. If you do, then you can expect God to increase your capabilities so you can use them to bless more people.

It Starts with Commitment

Taking your skills to the next level would not be possible without the commitment to do so. This commitment demands passion, time, effort, and consistency. However, when you see the outcome of your hard work, all your sacrifices will be worth it.

# CHAPTER 5

## DO NOT TAKE SHORTCUTS TO SUCCESS.

Be patient with the process of promotion, not just in the office, but in life overall. For instance, no matter how excited you are to earn bucks, do not quit school just so you can go to work already. Also, avoid under-the-table transactions, like bribing, just to get promoted at work, but rather work hard for that opportunity.

So many people are in such a hurry to success that they eagerly take any shortcuts that come across their way. In reality, shortcuts usually lead to disappointments rather than quicker success. The key to any long-term success is to take the necessary steps to steadily progress rather than skip any of them. This would be true whether the goals are financial or health or relationship related.
I've seen gullible people buy into the many 'get rich quick' or 'lose weight fast' schemes out there only to find out that

none of them work except in relieving you of the money paid for such products or programs. A friend of mine even bought one of those home devices that electronically stimulate belly muscle contractions thinking that weight lost is possible while watching TV. This friend, who did not want to put in the work of exercising in a gym, is still overweight today.

Shortcuts can result in loss of success As a certified ski instructor, I've seen many beginners who try to come down slopes that they are clearly not ready for. Such folks have not reached a level where they can consistently stop and turn on their skis while even on the bunny hill yet. For some reason, these same people ventured onto steeper slopes serviced by chairlifts and they end up frozen stiff with fear at the top.

I've had to physically climb back up a slope to rescue such novice skiers by holding them all the way safely back down the hill. Imagine how embarrassing this must be for an adult as this is how we usually start little three or four year-olds on the bunny hill.

If they do manage to start coming down on their own, they will usually panic, lose their focus and end up going straight down the hill with increasing speed. Of course a 'yard sale' (a ski phrase which describes a fallen skier with skis and poles ending up all over the slope) will be the result.

We always tell beginners that they must be completely comfortable in making solid turns and stops on a bunny hill before going onto slopes serviced by chairlifts. This is achieved only by extra practice outside of lesson time. But some are just impatient and decide to go on the chairlifts anyway before they are proficient on the easier slopes.

They thought that they could take shortcuts and bypass the steps required. Imagine the shock when they realize that even the easier slopes serviced by the chairlifts are way beyond their abilities and comfort levels when they are looking down these larger hills compared to the relatively flat bunny slopes.

Unfortunately, some of these beginners may never put on skis again because of their terrifying experiences. This is a real shame since they did make the initial efforts to come out to try skiing as a way to embrace winter. If they do come back to try again, sometimes it is the following winter when they have already loss the momentum of any progress as they have forgotten the basic skills.

The shortcuts they thought they could get away with resulted in a loss of success. These poor folks usually have to start all over again from scratch in terms of learning how to ski even the bunny hills. Their initial fears will take twice as much work to get over compared to those who did not take shortcuts in their learning.

Take the same steps as other successful people have done
Although it is wise to get proper coaching, instruction and mentoring for your goals, these are not considered shortcuts. They

are just more efficient ways to learn the skills required for success. However, time with a coach or instructor does not replace the steps one must take in order to be successful.

You still have to do your part of the work whether it's working out at the gym, building wealth, starting a new relationship or practicing your ski turns on the bunny hill. The bottom line is that there are no true shortcuts to real success.

Many of the goals we want to achieve have already been achieved by countless numbers of other people. Follow their examples and take the same type of steps they had to take in order to be successful. Each step is very much like a little success on its own and little successes do add up. Pay your dues to steadily develop towards success rather than take detours on shortcuts that can actually set you back.

# CHAPTER 6

## BE WILLING TO START FROM THE BOTTOM.

It is okay to start at the lowest position in a company. As you work hard up, you will learn a lot about the nature of your career, and you can use those learning to be an effective leader once you are at the top.

Why it's good to start at the bottom

t's good to start at the bottom. In fact, it can be a very good place to start when you're building your career.Whether you're interning or starting your first graduate job, the idea of starting from scratch, just when you've fought so hard to clamber up the academic ladder, can prove somewhat disheartening. Potentially even more so when you enter a workplace and you see things done, well frankly, not very well.

Today we're frequently reminded that 'the world is your oyster.' As such, should we find ourselves undertaking a mundane task or learning the ropes of an office job – even if this is by no means where we want to end up, the fact that we're having to do it at all, means we're somehow lacking in ambition or imagination. Consequently, one finds themselves plunged into something of an existential crisis. And that is never a good place to be. Trust me, I've been there.

In truth however, starting at the bottom or near to it can in fact be an exceptionally good place to start. Because learning from the ground up can teach you a lot. And I am not just saying that. I started at the bottom and while that was quite a few years ago now, I am rather glad I did. Firstly, basic administration is at the heart of all businesses and whether you like it or not, no matter where your career takes you, you'll always have an element of admin as part of your role.

You'll also always have a fair amount of admin to sort in your general life – and so acquiring the organisation skills to handle this will stand you in good stead.

Secondly, never underestimate just how much an office and its colleagues value the person who can fix the printer or order a courier to drop off some vital work to a client. Such seemingly basic, indeed boring nuggets of knowledge actually form the bedrock of day-to-day office life – and as you develop over the years that knowledge will make you stronger professionally.

No job should ever be beneath you – and the moment you think it is, it's perhaps the time to question whether you're becoming the kind of colleague, member of staff or indeed leader that you want to be. No matter at what stage your career might be, if you've had experience of doing the mundane, you'll appreciate and above all value that role, its function and what part it has to play in the role of business.

Consider this example, from the world of corporate law... Just before a deal is closed, the two sides have to agree on what information the seller has given to the buyer about what has been sold, be it a building, business or Boeing-747. This task often falls to the trainees, who will go through reems of folders to make sure that the paperwork matches on both sides.

Going through long documents, page by page, often late at night, is not what dreams are made of. However this is one of the most vital things to do before your client signs a multi-million dollar deal. A mismatch could cost either side a lot of money.

Fast-forward 20-odd years. Imagine it's your business that's being sold or you're the lead partner on the deal. The trainees still have to check all of the disclosed information but, having been there yourself, you'll understand what's involved and factor into the deal timetable enough time for them to do their job properly, thereby minimizing the risk to you or your client. Now that can only be good for business.

So never be afraid to start at the bottom because you never know when you'll be at the top.

*The Power of Starting From the Bottom:
Why Being Disadvantaged Is Your Biggest
Strength*

Rarely, if ever, do you hear someone who is wildly successful state that their formal education or personal connections to funding early on were what made them successful.

No one can argue that these things make a difference. But at the end of the day, when asked what were those qualities and advantages that really made the difference, what really allowed them to realize success, it's all those things you cultivate when you're in the furnace– without money or resources…only that deep burning fire and the skills you developed while you persevered through the tough times.

Clearly, these skills and the degree to which you have or develop them is different for everyone. But these are some of the incredible skills and advantages I've found starting from the bottom gives us:

1. An unstoppable hunger

This is the first and most prominent advantage.

Everyone I've ever known who has grown up more privileged (this doesn't have to be money, it can mean connections in the profession they decide to enter later on in life) didn't have the same hunger to accomplish their goals as someone that started from the bottom.

This isn't to say that anything, in particular, is required to realize success or that someone else is more entitled to success because they suffered more. Everyone should have the same chance to fulfill their dreams.

However, I know how hard you need to work and how much you need to be willing to sacrifice to really make your dreams happen. The truth is, you're just very unlikely to be successful unless you have a pure-burning, unstoppable hunger that tends to only come from the adversity you experience when starting from the bottom.

2. A scrappiness that refines your resourcefulness

Resourcefulness is a skill that is highly valued by some of the world's most successful, including Amazon.com founder, Jeff Bezos.

The thing with resourcefulness is, it's essentially your problem-solving ability, and you can't solve problems if you don't have any.

The great thing is anyone can throw themselves into the fire and start a business or pursue their passion. And when you do that, you're often forced to solve a myriad of problems just to help your efforts survive in the first few years. This kind of scrappiness you develop by chasing your dreams refines your resourcefulness, a skill you'll continue to use as your dreams grow.

3. A compelling story that others will be attracted by and identify with

Less a skill or ability and more a part of who you are, by starting from the bottom and clawing your way up with your unstoppable hunger and scrappy problem solving, your story becomes an example of hope, a confirmation to others that you can realize your dreams, and something to believe in and follow.

Your story makes you someone and something that people want to follow and this holds several incredible advantages just within itself. Your efforts from here on out gather attention, they draw help, and they help propel anything and everything you ever do from that point on.

And that's all in addition to the people you'll help inspire to go after their own dreams and goals because they're also starting from the bottom and lack the confidence to believe they can do it.

Starting from the bottom is tough, no matter what your goals or dreams are. But the experiences we go through and the circumstances that surround us are a breeding ground for some of the most powerful and important ingredients for success.

If you're starting from the bottom, believe in yourself because you have advantages that others who don't have to start from the bottom will never have: an unstoppable hunger, the resourcefulness to make anything happen, and an inspiring story in the making that will fuel you and inspire others.

# CHAPTER 7

## LET GO OF BITTERNESS TOWARDS OTHERS.

If you have grudges against some people, then forgive and wish them well. Resentment can dull the heart and it can have an impact on how you perceive life and your desire to be successful. It will make you turn those who hurt you into unknowing rivals, and your motivation for achieving your goals will be to surpass them—which is not healthy.

*Strategies to let go of of bitterness towards others*

1. Recognize the source of your anger and bitterness.

<u>Recognize</u> when you are feeling angry and bitter towards others, and try to determine the cause. Is the cause something you can change or control, or is it out of your hands?

Further, is your anger being caused by someone who you will never see again, such as a grocery clerk or a server at a restaurant? Or is a family member or friend making you angry?

This is important to recognize because anger that you feel when dealing with people who are close to you involves an ongoing interaction. To handle these situations, the best strategies to implement are escaping the situation, relaxing, restructuring your thoughts, or expressing your anger directly in a calm and appropriate tone.

Another way to recognize the source of your anger is to step back and evaluate your life. Are you where you expected yourself to be at this point? It is possible that you are experiencing built-up frustration because your life is not meeting your expectations or you are not living up to the standards that you perceive other people have for you.

<u>Unhealthy relationships</u> and past experiences are also a common source of

anger. When one person is often feeling vulnerable, or is triggered by a past pain in their relationship, it can lead to feelings of anger to cover up this pain. If you can identify the past experience that is continuing to impact your life in a negative way, you have to face that situation head-on so you can let it go

2. Practice relaxation techniques.

Using simple relaxation strategies can help you soothe your angry feelings. If you practice these strategies often, you will find that it is easier to resort to them when you feel anger emerging. It is important to find which techniques work best for you to help you process your thoughts with a clearer mindset.

For example, many people enjoy aromatherapy to help them relax. Whether you use essential oils in a bath or in a diffuser, this is a great stress reliever and relaxation tool that is easily accessible. Another common technique is to listen to soothing music. This can help take your mind away from the situation at hand, and help you re-center your thoughts.

. Take a brief time out.

It is crucial to realize when it is time to take a minute for yourself. If you are doing something or talking to someone and you can sense that you have anger building up, simply excuse yourself. Walk away and take a few minutes to gather your thoughts and release the negative emotions. Take this time to think about how you want to respond before you speak.

Taking a timeout will prevent you from saying something out of anger that you might later regret. Find a quiet and relaxing place to go in case you need a break. Think about some things you could do to cool down during this time, such as slow, deep breathing and mindfulness exercises.

After your anger has subsided and before returning to the situation, consider what you will say when you return. For example, if you were talking to someone, express that you appreciate their understanding and thank them for giving you the chance to calm down.

4. Get daily exercise.

Getting physical exercise is one of the most effective ways to reduce your anger and stress. Physical exercise gives you a chance to release your emotions, so going for a walk or run every day can help calm you down in general. Exercise can also help increase the release of endorphins in your body, which will naturally make you feel better and reduce your stress levels.

<u>Finding a healthy hobby</u> such as exercising will relieve tension, as your mind will become occupied. Try a few things until you find something that you enjoy doing. This will help encourage you to take a break from your normal routine, and help you build your self-esteem.

5. Find workable solutions.

Instead of focusing on whatever triggered your anger, work on finding a solution to the issue at hand. Instead of staying angry, do something about it. For example, is your spouse late for dinner every night? Instead of facing this drama on a nightly basis, find a workable solution. Perhaps you can schedule meals for later in the evening, or the two of you can agree to eat on your own on certain nights.

You have to recognize the things that are out of your control, and understand that you cannot change them. Knowing what you can control will let you use your limited energy in the most effective way possible. The time you waste thinking about and trying to change situations that are out of your control could be spent on things that you *do* have control over, which would then allow you to make progress.

6. Don't hold grudges.

Holding grudges has <u>more health implications for you</u> than it does for the other person. Not only do they take up your energy, but they also make your emotional state toxic.

Even if you have been legitimately offended, which most people have, try to take an empathic perspective rather than acting like a victim. Forgiving thoughts will allow you to have a greater sense of perceived control and a reduced physiological stress response, which will help decrease your anger.

7. Practice forgiveness.

Forgiveness may look different for everyone, but it generally involves making an active decision to let go of resentful feelings and thoughts of revenge. Once this is done, your anger will no longer drain your energy, and you will be able to have peace of mind.

The act that hurt you may always be with you, but forgiveness will set you free from the control of the incident or person who caused you harm. When you are able to forgive someone else, you are not doing it for their sake. Rather, you are doing it so you can regain control of your life and move on. This doesn't mean that you are forgetting or excusing the harmful behavior, but it will bring you some peace.

8. Own your anger.

You need to learn how to control your anger before it starts to control you. To do this, acknowledge when you're angry, and remind yourself that you can get over it. Remember that the feeling won't last, and it will only get as bad as you allow it to.

The logic of our emotions does not always make sense. For example, if you were hurt as a child by a parent and you are still holding onto that anger as an adult and waiting for someone else to fix it for you, you are never going to get over it. You have to realize that it is up to you to <u>own your anger</u> and address it in order to move on. You are the only person who is in control of your feelings.

9. Talk to a friend.

Reach out to a trusted friend who you know will give you their full attention. Let out your anger and frustrations to them and get their feedback. Often, when a friend knows you well, they can provide the best advice for you that can fit in with your life. A good friend may be able to reframe a situation for you and get you to see it in a different light.

It also feels good to vent. Sometimes you just need to talk something through to someone who is willing to listen, so you can get your feelings out. It might be a good idea to set some boundaries for your venting. For example, ask your friend if you can have five minutes to talk... and then only give yourself *five* minutes. Pay attention to the number of times you repeat yourself, and you will likely find that you do this a lot in order to provide emphasis. Set limits to ensure you keep it brief, sort out your thoughts, and focus on a solution.

10. Recite positive affirmations.

Recurring anger is an affirmation. You need to replace these negative affirmations with <u>positive ones</u>. You can choose to think in a way that creates a negative mental atmosphere, or you can choose to think in a way that helps develop a healthy atmosphere for you and the people around you.

Tell yourself that you are in control and no one can make you feel inferior. Doing this will help calm you down if you are beginning to feel yourself getting angry. Learn to practice both present and future affirmations so you can use this technique to prevent anger, and to deal with it in the moment when it is occurring.

11. Express yourself in a journal

Writing about your anger in a journal is one of the most effective ways to express and understand your feelings. <u>Through writing</u>, you can process your thoughts carefully.

Once you identify the root causes of your anger, you will have the control you need to analyze your responses. Writing about your anger will help you learn from it and take positive action to protect yourself in the future by increasing your self-awareness.

Some people choose to draw or paint what they are feeling instead of writing it down in words. This is also an effective method of journaling. Draw what your anger looks like to you, and express yourself in a creative way to help yourself move on.

12. Change your environment.

Sometimes your immediate surroundings are causing you irritation. Problems may begin to weigh you down and make you feel trapped. You can escape this by making sure you set aside personal time.

Elements in your environment may be making you more likely to get angry. For example, if you find that you often get angry in the mornings when you are rushing around and trying to get everyone up and ready for the day, try to find a way to reduce this stress the night before so you can lighten your load in the morning.

Alternatively, if you have been in a relationship that has gone sour, avoid doing anything that reminds you of the person who hurt you. This includes not going to places where you used to go together, and even not listening to songs that remind you of that person. You might need to find alternate routes to work or school to bypass areas that remind you of this person, and recreate your routine to avoid negative thoughts.

13. Become more self-aware.

Becoming more <u>self-aware</u> can help you prevent your anger from happening. Becoming aware of your false beliefs requires introspective work, including developing the skills to pay attention to your mind and dissect some of your negative thoughts. Once you become aware of what triggers your anger, you can apply your techniques to change the dynamics that are going on in your mind and causing your emotions.

If you are able to embrace yourself and avoid a victim mentality, the results of your self-awareness practices can lead to a permanent change. By becoming self-aware, you can identify the primary elements or feelings that trigger your anger, such as fear or pain.

14. Laugh.

Can you think of an experience you have had where you ended up laughing at something that made you mad? This moment can be transformational because humor is both healing and empowering. If you are able to laugh about something, you are able to gain power over it instead of allowing it to have power over you.

If you can't find any humor in the situation that is making you angry, turn to things that you know will make you laugh, and get into this positive frame of mind. For example, you can watch a funny movie or video, or meet up with a friend who always makes you laugh. This is a good way to change your mindset and get your mind off of whatever is making you angry.

15. Take deep breaths.

Stopping to take intentional deep breaths will force you to calm down. Stop what you are doing and count down from three while inhaling, hold it for five seconds, and then exhale. This will help you take a moment before reacting to something irrationally.

For example, imagine someone just cut you off in traffic and you can feel yourself becoming enraged. Instead of immediately reacting, take a moment for some deep and intentional breaths. This will give your body a chance to calm down, and it will give you time to think twice about how you react.

16. Use a stress-relief tool.

Stress-relief tools and toys can be used as preventative measures, or in the moment to calm you down. If you can turn your focus onto something you are playing with, or channel your aggression into a physical object, you may be able to reduce your feelings of anger.

17. Avoid the person who causes you pain.

If it is possible, avoid coming into contact with the person who caused you pain. Instead, surround yourself with people who lift you up and empower you to feel good about yourself. Take control over your emotions by not allowing other people to impact them, and avoiding being around people who try to negatively affect your feelings.

After having a bad experience, avoid saying "never" and "always." Instead, try to isolate your bad experience and realize that there are no absolutes. Sure, something may happen more than once, and you want to acknowledge that—but using words like *never* and *always* is not a rational way of thinking.

18. Be assertive.

<u>Being assertive</u> is an important communication skill that is very different from being aggressive. When you are assertive, you are clearly expressing yourself and defending your point of view, while still respecting other people's beliefs.

Assertive communication can help you earn the respect of other people and boost your self-esteem. It shows that you are confident in what you are talking about, and are willing to stand your ground while still maintaining self-control.

 This can help reduce stress because you will know that you have clearly expressed your wants or needs to another person. In order to start being assertive, learn to say what you mean and mean what you say.

19. Don't sweat the small stuff.

Do you ever find that you are giving up happiness for minor inconveniences that are out of your control?

Your happiness is largely impacted by your ability to let things go, and to realize what you can and can't control.

When something happens, your initial feelings of anger are natural and unavoidable because they are created by chemical reactions in your body. But those chemicals last only about six seconds.

Anything that happens after that is due to your own decision to ruminate.

# CHAPTER 8

## SURROUND YOURSELF WITH SUCCESSFUL PEOPLE.

The people you usually spend time with have an influence on how you think and behave. As the author and motivational speaker, Jim Rohn, said, *"You are the average of the five people you spend the most time with."* Therefore, if you want to have the mindset of an achiever, then be surrounded by achievers.

*HOW TO SURROUND YOURSELF WITH SUCCESSFUL PEOPLE*

We all want success – in our business, in our finances, in our relationships. So why do so few people actually find fulfillment in all of these areas?

The answer lies in your standards.

"The only thing that will change your life, change your business, change your relationship, is that you must raise your standards," Tony says. Get rid of negative people who bring you down. Surround yourself with people who lift you up, lend you knowledge and help you learn from your mistakes. Raise your standards for your inner circle.

This concept is also called the law of attraction, and it goes back at least to Confucius in the 6th century BC, who wrote one of the first quotes about surrounding yourself with good people: "If you are the smartest person in the room, then you are in the wrong room." The idea that you are who you surround yourself with has lasted this long because it's true – and you can use it to achieve your dreams in business and in life.

## *WHY IS IT IMPORTANT TO SURROUND YOURSELF WITH GOOD PEOPLE?*

Have you ever heard someone say, "You are who you hang out with?" If you have kids, you likely worry about them falling in with the wrong crowd – and your parents worried the same for you. That's because those you spend the most time with have a huge influence on your moods, how you view the world and the expectations you have of yourself. As parents, we instinctively know this, and we want to use this power of proximity to have a positive effect on our children. So why don't we also use it to our own advantage?

Surrounding yourself with good people can affect every aspect of your life, from business to romantic relationships. When you surround yourself with positivity, you're more likely to adopt empowering beliefs **and see** life as happening for you instead of to you. Just as you benefit when you surround yourself with people who make you happy, you suffer when those in your business or social circles are negative or narrow-minded.

## *HOW TO SURROUND YOURSELF WITH GOOD PEOPLE*

Proximity is power: Always remember that who you spend the most time with is who you eventually become. To reach new heights of success, you must surround yourself with people who not only inspire you, but challenge you. It isn't always easy, but it's worth it.

## 1. DECIDE TO SURROUND YOURSELF WITH GREATNESS

We all have goals in our lives, but which objectives are *musts* in your book? The pursuits you choose to invest time in are a reflection of your standards, and so are your relationships. Are you trying to grow your business? If so, then why would you choose to hang around people who bring negativity and distraction into your life? The number one way to begin to surround yourself with positivity is to make the decision, right now, that you are going to raise your standards.

Maybe you've just gotten used to having certain people around or are worried about moving on. Don't let fear ruin your life. When you actively choose to surround yourself with people who make you happy and who share your ambitions, it elevates the standard of what you will or won't tolerate in your business and your life. Your goals and dreams are worth it – once you believe that, you'll be unstoppable.

## 2. LET GO OF NEGATIVE RELATIONSHIPS

Do you consider yourself a go-getter, yet your business partners and team lack ambition? Are you searching for that next level of success, but are being held back by those around you? Identifying the people in your life who are bringing you down is the first step in making shifts to your peer group or colleagues. Letting go of negative relationships will allow you more time to surround yourself with successful people.

The best way to determine who these individuals are is to think about how you feel after spending time with them. Do you feel good about yourself and ready to take on new challenges? Or do you feel upset, unsure of yourself and not in control of your emotions? Our emotions exist to tell us things – they're a gift that lets us know what we need to change in order to feel more fulfilled. If you feel drained, fearful or agitated after spending time with someone, it's a sign they aren't good for you.

It can often be uncomfortable to step away from relationships that are lacking. You don't want to burn bridges, and you might have known some of these friends or colleagues for a long time. But it's essential not to feel obligated because they are "old friends" or feel that you owe them something. Determine what's driving your decision to stay in these relationships, so that you can change your mindset and free yourself. You'll be more prepared to focus on what really matters to you and your business.

## 3. IDENTIFY POSITIVE PEOPLE

Just as you likely have negative relationships in your life, you probably already have some positive people in your corner as well. They don't all have to be the same – in fact, you'll benefit from having a diverse range of personality types within your group. These four types of people are good to have in your inner circle when you need to surround yourself with positivity.

- Smart people. Surrounding yourself with people who are smarter than you will push you to always keep learning and to stay curious – two essential traits of those who eventually succeed in business.
- Hard workers. Success is about more than smarts – in fact, there are plenty of smart people out there who don't

have the drive to succeed. The hunger of a hard worker inspires everyone around them to do more, be more and achieve more.

. Dreamers and visionaries. The world needs dreamers as much as it needs doers. The visionary in your circle is the one who will entertain your wildest ideas and always encourage you to chase your dreams.

. Positive thinkers. No one is happy all of the time, but there are those who see obstacles as opportunities and those who see them as insurmountable roadblocks. When the going gets tough, you want the first type of person in your life.

## 4. JOIN A PROFESSIONAL GROUP

If you want to accelerate your success, it's important to surround yourself with people you can learn from. Finding a mentor is an excellent way to surround yourself with successful people – Tony will tell you that no one does it alone and that he himself had many mentors throughout his life. A mentor is someone who is already getting the results you want. They have a strategy for success, whether they know it or not, and by spending time with them you can develop a similar one. How does this person respond to conflict? How do they network and forge relationships with key contacts? What habits have they established that lead to their greatness? Observe their patterns and see how you can adapt similar ones into your life.

You can also join a mastermind group or another professional group, either online or in person, or work with a business coach who can help you overcome limiting beliefs and seek out uplifting people to spend time around. Not only will the coach be a good person to spend time with, they'll also be able to help you identify which individuals in your life to limit your exposure to and help you seek out new venues for forging beneficial relationships.

## 5. GET OUTSIDE YOUR COMFORT ZONE

As Tony says, "All growth starts at the end of your comfort zone." To surround yourself with good people who will take you to the next level, you need to spend time where they are. Ambitious people attend seminars and workshops that feed their minds and cause them to stretch themselves. They expose themselves to those with different perspectives and continually push themselves out of their comfort zones.

Tony Robbins has spent decades working with top business leaders and influencers throughout various industries. By surrounding himself with the best in the business world, Tony has been able to learn the strategies necessary for any business to thrive. At Business Mastery, the five-day event that will transform your business, you will be surrounded by world-class speakers and like-minded individuals who are hungry to succeed.

Hear from experts and meet others like yourself who are searching for the knowledge needed to take their businesses to the next level. By bringing success into your life and attending Business Mastery, you not only gain exposure to some of the most hardworking, driven people in the world, but you recognize that your dreams are worth fighting for.

## GO FOR IT

With determination and hard work, nothing is impossible for you to achieve. Just give your best and never give up, even when it gets tough. Someday, you will get what you are aiming for.